THE ULTIMATE CLAY BEAD BOOK

by the Editors of Klutz

KLUTZ®

KLUTZ® creates activity books and other great stuff for kids ages 3 to 103. We began our corporate life in 1977 in a garage we shared with a Chevrolet Impala. Although we've outgrown that first office, Klutz galactic headquarters is still staffed entirely by real human beings. For those of you who collect mission statements, here's ours:

CREATE WONDERFUL THINGS
BE YOURSELF · HAVE FUN

WRITE US
We would love to hear your comments regarding this or any of our books.
KLUTZ®
557 Broadway
New York, NY 10012
thefolks@klutz.com

Distributed in the UK by
Scholastic UK Ltd
No 1 London Bridge
London, SE1 9BG
United Kingdom

Distributed in Canada by
Scholastic Canada Ltd
604 King Street West
Toronto, Ontario
Canada M5V 1E1

Distributed in Australia by
Scholastic Australia Ltd
PO Box 579
Gosford, NSW
Australia 2250

Distributed in Hong Kong
by Scholastic
Hong Kong Ltd
Suites 2001-2
Top Glory Tower
262 Gloucester Road
Causeway Bay, Hong Kong

Distributed in the
European Union by
Scholastic Ltd
Unit 89E, Lagan Road
Dublin Industrial Estate
Glasnevin, Dublin 11
Ireland

ISBN 978-1-338-89603-9
4 1 5 8 5 7 0 8 8 8

FSC
www.fsc.org
MIX
Paper from
responsible sources
FSC® C119793

This product is made of FSC®-certified and other controlled material. FSC® is dedicated to the promotion of responsible forest management worldwide.

Stock photos ©Shutterstock.com

SAFETY ADVICE FOR CLAY WARNING

Not suitable for children under 8 years. For use under adult supervision. Read the instructions before use, follow them, and keep them for reference.

ADVICE FOR ADULT SUPERVISION

- Read and follow these instructions, safety rules, and first aid information, and keep them for reference.
- Not suitable for children under 8 years. For use under adult supervision. Keep this set out of reach of children under 8 years old.
- Supervising adults should exercise discretion as to which activities are suitable and safe for children.
- The supervising adult should discuss the instructions and safety information with children before crafting.
- Incorrect use of chemicals can cause injury and damage to health. Only carry out those activities that are listed in the instructions.
- The baking area should be well lit and ventilated and close to a water supply. When projects are removed from the oven, they should be placed on a heat-resistant counter or surface.
- Protect work surface. Clay may stain or damage finished surfaces.
- Clay can be disposed of with normal refuse (household rubbish).

SAFETY RULES

- Do not eat, drink, or smoke in the activity area.
- For ages 8 and up; store clay out of reach of children under the specified age limit and animals and keep them away from the activity area.
- It is best to craft in a clear area, away from food or drinks. Do not eat, drink, or smoke in the activity area.
- Do not exceed a temperature of 260°F (125°C). If baked at higher temperatures, the clay can release fumes that may irritate your eyes.
- The baking process is not part of the function of the toy and should be carried out by the supervising adult.
- Use a domestic oven thermometer, e.g, bimetal, to measure the temperature. Do not use a glass thermometer.
- Use only the tools that come with the kit or are recommended in the instructions.
- Do not heat the material and cook food at the same time in a domestic oven.
- Do not exceed a baking time of 30 minutes or the clay could burn.
- Do not use a microwave oven.
- Wash hands after crafting.
- Clean all equipment after use.
- Do not put the clay in your mouth or ingest the clay.
- If the glass bottle breaks, be sure to clean up the area immediately and discard all broken pieces.

FIRST AID INFORMATION

- In case of injury: Always seek medical advice.
- In case of accidental overheating and inhalation of poisonous gases: Remove person to fresh air and seek immediate medical advice.
- In case of doubt, seek medical advice without delay. Take the chemical and/or product together with the container with you.

Contents

SHAPES 10

DISC
10

SQUARE
10

STAR
10

TRIANGLE
11

ADDING TEXTURE
12

ADDING STRIPES
13

SMILEY FACE
14

PEACE SIGN
15

LETTERS
16

POLKA DOTS
18

COW PRINT
19

TERRAZZO
20

MARBLING
21

RAINBOW
22

BEES
23

CANES 24

FLOWERS
24

SPIRAL
25

MILLEFIORI
26

CHECKERBOARD
28

MAKING YOUR BRACELET
30

PROJECT IDEAS
32

WHAT YOU GET

Everything you need to make dozens of clay beads!

CLAY IN 9 COLORS

**FAUX PEARL
SPACER BEADS**

**ELASTIC CORD IN
3 COLORS**

PROJECT SUPPLIES
Use these to finish your projects.
Check out some ideas on page 32.

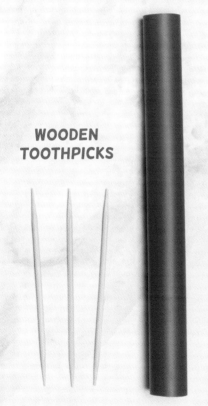

CLAY-SCULPTING TOOLS
These will help you sculpt the clay.

METAL AWL FOR MAKING HOLES

ROLLER

WOODEN TOOTHPICKS

Cutting blade

SPATULA

Flattening side

Pointy end

SET UP YOUR CRAFT STATION

- It's best to work on a table that's been covered with tin foil, parchment paper, scrap paper, or an inexpensive tablecloth. (Don't use the fine linens for crafting!)

- Don't leave your unbaked clay on any furniture. Unbaked clay can "leak" if it's left out too long. Always wrap up your clay in plastic cling film or baggies when you're done crafting.

- Grab the most responsible grown-up in calling distance when you're ready to bake your projects in the oven. Grown-ups seem to appreciate it when you have a LOT of beads to bake at once, rather than cooking 'em one at a time.

- Grown-ups should always manage the baking process (page 8). Remind them to use oven mitts.

- Never touch the clay or the metal awl until it's finished cooling. We recommend giving it a good hour. (Use the time to tidy up your craft station.) Handle the metal awl and the baking sheet with oven mitts or hot pads just in case you forget to let it cool completely.

Basic Bead

Start here! Grab some clay and start rolling.

TIP Many of the projects in this book will have a size guide to match the beads in this book. But you can make the beads bigger or smaller.

Roll Your Clay

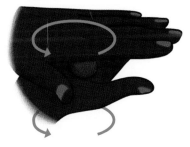

1 Tear off a small piece of clay, about this size.

2 Place the clay between the palms of your hands. Spin your hands in opposite directions. Your hunk of clay will gradually form into a round ball.

TA-DA! It's a round sphere (also called a ball).

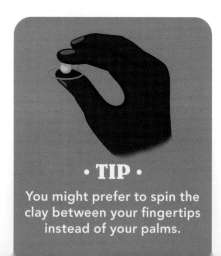

· TIP ·
You might prefer to spin the clay between your fingertips instead of your palms.

6

Make a Hole

3 Now gently hold your clay in one hand. With the other hand, hold the metal awl.

4 Carefully poke the awl into the clay. Twist the awl in your fingers as you pierce the clay.

TIP

Work slowly! The clay can mush or get out of shape if you rush.

5 For a neater look, push the awl in the opposite direction.

6 You can remove the awl before you bake OR you can make a lot of beads and keep them all on the oven-safe awl.

YOU'RE NOT DONE YET!
Keep going to the next stage.

Baking Clay

Got some projects ready for the oven? Here's how to bake them.

Prepping Your Beads

Leave the clay on the metal awl while you bake it. This helps the bead keep its shape, so it's easier to thread the cord through it at the end.

You can leave multiple beads on the awl. Just make sure there's a little space between the clay. If a clay bead is touching another clay bead, they might fuse together in the oven.

Did You Know?

Humans have been making beads for a long, long time. The oldest known beads were made of seashells, about 100,000 years ago!

1 Find a responsible, grown-up assistant to handle the baking process.

2 Preheat your oven to 250°F (120°C). You can use a full-size oven or a toaster oven.

3 Smooth some aluminum foil over a cookie sheet. Place your projects on the foil. Then put the cookie sheet in the oven.

Balancing Your Beads

If your beads are flat (like the peace sign and smiley face), you can place them flat on your cookie sheet covered with foil.

If you have a narrow baking sheet (like a loaf pan), you can balance the needle on the edges.

Or on the cookie sheet, scrunch up balls of foil to rest each end of your needle on.

4 Bake your projects for 5–10 minutes. Bitty beads will bake more quickly than bigger beads.

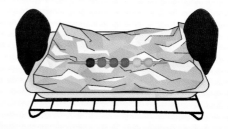

5 Using oven mitts, take the cookie sheet out of the oven. Place it on a heat-safe surface or a cooling rack.

Safety Stuff

- Always use oven mitts to take your projects out of the oven.

- Always let the needle cool down. It's made of metal so it will stay hot for awhile. Give it a good hour of cool-down time.

- Never put plastic in the oven. Your plastic spatula, roller, and pearl beads are not designed to go into the oven.

SHAPES

Use the spatula to make your basic bead into other shapes. It's best to make your shape first. Then pierce it with the needle.

Disc

1 Flatten a ball of clay slightly. You can use your thumb . . .

. . . or the flat side of the spatula.

2 Stand the shape on its edge. Roll the shape gently on the table to make a firmer edge.

Square

1 Press the flat side of the spatula on a ball of clay. This creates two flat sides.

2 Then turn the clay and press again. Repeat this action until you have six flat sides, just like a cube.

Star

1 Press the clay into a thick pancake.

2 Pinch the edges of the pancake between your fingertips. Rotate the clay and pinch it again to make five points.

3 Keep shaping the points with your fingertips until they look pretty even.

Triangle

1 Roll a ball of clay. (Don't pierce it yet.)

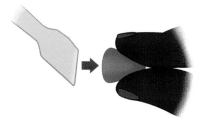

2 Pinch the ball between your thumb and pointer finger. This creates two flattish sides.

3 Then press the flat side of the spatula against the rounded side.

4 Finally, use the flat side of the spatula again to straighten the triangle's sides. Flatten the top and bottom, too, until all the sides look flat.

Once your shape is done, you can make a hole (page 7) with the metal awl.

MAKE SURE YOUR BEAD IS AT LEAST THIS THICK. THINNER BEADS MIGHT NOT FIT ON THE AWL.

Chill Out!

- Are your beads too smooshy? Chilling them will make the clay a little easier to pierce with the metal awl while keeping their shape.

- Put your clay pieces on a foil-lined cookie sheet or a paper plate. Then stick them in the freezer or the fridge for a few hours. Label your work so no one in your house mistakes the clay for food.

Adding Texture

Use the tools to poke dots and lines into your shapes.

POKE-A-DOTS

Use the pointy end of the spatula to press dents all over the bead.

TINY POKE-A-DOTS

Use the pointy end of the metal awl. Or a toothpick.

DAISY

Press the side of the awl around the edges of a disc.

Add a tiny ball of clay with dots to the center.

TOTALLY TUBULAR

While your bead is on the awl, press the side of the toothpick all the way around the clay.

ADDING STRIPES

Jazz up your basic beads with rainbow stripes!

1 Roll a small ball of clay back and forth on your work surface.

2 Keep rolling! The clay will turn into a snake. Repeat with as many colors as you want.

3 Lightly drape the thin stripes across your bead. Cut off any extra with the blade end of the spatula.

4 If your bead is . . .

ROUND

Gently roll the bead between your hands to make the stripes smooth and flat.

ANOTHER SHAPE

Gently press the stripes to your bead with the flat end of the spatula. Cut off any extra clay with your blade.

Smiley Face

SIZE GUIDE

❏ Bead ❏ Stripe

Get happy and make a groovy 1960s icon.

1 Flatten a ball into a disc. (Check out page 10 for tips.)

2 With the pointy end of the spatula, carve eyes and a smile on one side of the disc.

3 Then roll super-thin stripes with black clay (page 13).

4 Cut the stripes with the blade end of the tool and fit them into the smile line you made.

5 Add two tiny dots for eyes. Flatten everything a little with the flat side of your spatula.

6 Make a hole (page 7) using the metal awl.

What's your mood?

SAD   ANGRY   OUT OF THIS WORLD

PEACE SIGN

1 Start by making a disc. (Follow the steps on page 10.)

2 Roll super-thin stripes in a different color.

3 Wrap a long stripe around the edge of the disc.

4 Add two or three short stripes to make the peace sign. Use the flat side of the spatula to gently press the stripes down.

Pop Quiz!

QUESTION:
The iconic smiley face, favored by hippies in the 1960s and alternative rock bands in the 1990s, was originally created for what kind of advertising campaign?

A. Movie studio

B. Chocolate chip cookie bakery

C. Insurance company

Answer: An insurance company. How square!

LETTERS

Say it loud and proud!
Write out your name or a
favorite word in clay.

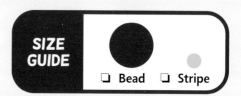

SIZE GUIDE

❑ Bead ❑ Stripe

1 Make a disc for each letter in your name or word.

2 Roll super-thin stripes (page 13) and cut them into pieces.

3 Lay the stripes on the front of the disc in the shape of each letter.

CREATE WONDERFUL THINGS

I ♥ Beads!

STACK 'EM ANY WAY YOU LIKE!

Tiny balls of clay make great spacer beads.

POLKA DOTS

Seeing spots? This playful pattern is easier than it looks.

YOU'LL NEED
- Ball
- Dots

1 Stick little balls onto your ball and then roll the entire ball between your hands.

2 Make a hole with the metal awl (page 7).

Cow Print

YOU'LL NEED
- Ball
- Blobs

1 Smoosh the blobs flattish and stretch them to make irregular shapes.

2 Place the flattened blobs around the bead.

3 Cluster a couple of small balls together in one spot.

4 Roll it smooth. Then make a hole with the metal awl.

Clouds
White blobs on a blue bead look like puffy clouds.

Terrazzo

Make a mosaic of leftover scraps into something new!

1 Stick little scraps all around the bead.

TIP

This is a great project to use with leftovers, after you've made other beads.

Your terrazzo beads don't need to be round. Try out squares, triangles, or even stars. (Check out page 10 for the how-to.)

2 Roll the ball smooth.

3 Pierce a hole through the center with the awl.

Did You Know?

Terrazzo is a type of mosaic made with chips of different stone poured into the pavement. The Hollywood Walk of Fame stars are made with terrazzo.

MARBLING

Twist and roll! This is a great way to use up scraps from other projects. Or if you don't like a bead you've already made, smoosh it into a marble bead instead.

YOU'LL NEED
■ Scraps

1 Roll out your clay into a thick stripe. Use at least two colors.

2 Twist the colors together in opposite directions.

3 Scrunch up the twist. (There's no wrong way to do this.)

4 Roll it out into a snake again. Fold it in half. Then twist.

5 Scrunch up the twist. Then roll it into a smooth ball.

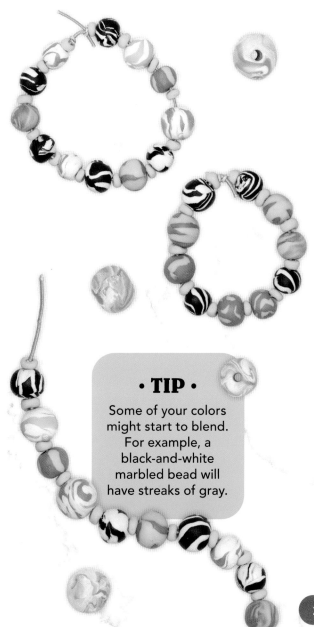

· TIP ·
Some of your colors might start to blend. For example, a black-and-white marbled bead will have streaks of gray.

RAINBOW

The extra-big bead looks cool as the center of your necklace or bracelet.

YOU'LL NEED
- Clay in 7 colors
- Ball

SIZE GUIDE

1 Roll out a snake in every color.

2 Bend the purple snake into an arc.

3 Stack the stripes in rainbow-color order.

4 Use the roller to gently roll across the rainbow.

5 Smoosh the ball to the back of the rainbow.

6 Use the metal awl to make a hole through the bead.

Did You Know?

If you're lucky enough to see a double rainbow, the second rainbow will have the colors in reverse!

Bee

SIZE GUIDE

- ❏ Ball
- ❏ Stripe
- ❏ Head
- ❏ Wings

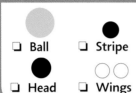

TIP

Wash your hands in between colors to avoid smudges.

1   Add a black stripe to the center of the yellow ball. You can roll the ball again to smooth out the stripe.

2   Place the head on one yellow end of the ball.

3   Pierce the metal awl through the head and out the other side of the yellow.

4   Flatten the wings into discs. Then pinch one end to make a teardrop. Press the wings flat onto the striped part of the bead.

CANES

A neat trick to make lots of beads with the same design!

Fl wers

Harness the power of flowers!

SIZE GUIDE

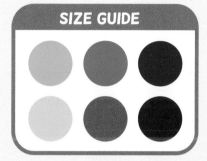

1 Roll each color into a short snake, about the same length.

2 Press five different snakes of clay around your center color.

3 Gently roll the bundle of clay together.

4 Follow Steps 5–7 of the Spiral (page 25) to slice your clay into discs.

Spiral

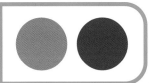

These swirly two-tone beads are a great way to learn the basics of making canes.

SIZE GUIDE

1 Roll two colors of clay into flat circles.

2 Stack one piece of clay on the other. (The bottom clay will be the outside of your bead.)

3 Use the blade to cut the circle into a square.

4 Starting at one end, roll up the clay tight like a jelly roll.

5 Put the cane in a fridge or freezer to firm up the clay.

6 Then slice the jelly roll into flat discs. Scoot the blade back and forth so the cane rolls as you cut.

7 Finally, pierce each flat disc with the metal awl.

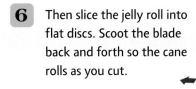

• TIP •

Freeze your clay before you cut to help the beads hold their shape. You can also ask a grown-up to use a super-sharp craft knife instead of your clay tool.

TIP

The ends of the cane always look smooshed. You can use the scraps to make terrazzo or marbled beads (page 20).

Millefiori

The word *millefiori* (MILL-eh-fee-OR-ee) is Italian for "thousand flowers." Artists have made millefiori-style mosaic patterns for thousands of years!

SIZE GUIDE

❑ Core ❑ Wrap ❑ Center

1 Roll the core into a snake.

2 Flatten the wrap color into a disc. Then use the roller to roll it flat.

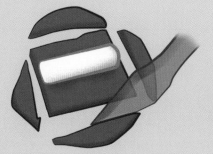

3 Place the core on the wrap. Cut the wrap clay into a square.

4 Wrap the square around the core. If you have extra wrap clay, cut it off.

5 Roll the clay into a long snake. Cut the snake into 6 equal lengths.

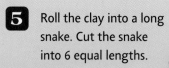

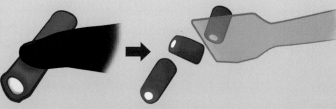

Megafiori

Once you have a bunch of millefiori discs, you can place them around a large bead.

6 Repeat Step 1 with the center. Then bundle the wrapped pieces around the center.

7 Roll the bundle together on the table to make a smooth cane.

8 Follows Steps 5–7 from the Spiral (page 25) to freeze and slice your clay into discs.

Did You Know?

Glass artists in medieval Italy were famous for using the *millefiori* technique. Glass-making also uses a lot of fire! Because townspeople worried about their buildings catching fire, the glass makers created their own artists' community on an island called Murano.

Checkerboard

Skater-cool style!

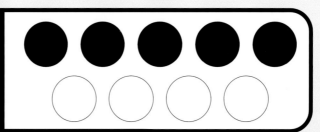

SIZE
GUIDE

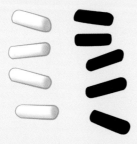

1 Roll all your clay into snakes of equal lengths.

2 Use the flat end of your spatula to flatten each snake.

3 Then turn each snake onto the round side and flatten them again.

4 This creates 9 rectangular snakes.

5 Layer three rectangles in an alternating pattern, with Color #2 in the middle.

TIP
Lightly roll the roller over each layer as you build them up.

The checkerboards won't be perfectly straight. That's what makes them cool and handmade!

6 Then stack two more layers, alternating the colors.

7 Roll each side flat with the roller to make a longer block, until it's about as wide as you want your beads to be.

8 Follows Steps 5–7 of the Spiral (page 25) to freeze and slice your beads.

USE YOUR SCRAPS FROM THIS PROJECT TO MAKE TERRAZZO AND MARBLED BEADS (PAGES 20–21).

Making Your Bracelet

YOU'LL NEED
- Baked, cooled beads (page 8)
- Elastic cord
- Faux-pearl spacer beads (optional)

1 Measure your wrist with the elastic cord. Don't cut it yet! You'll want extra space for tying the knot.

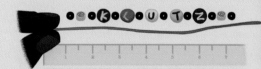

2 Place the elastic on the table and arrange the beads how you want them. (Or you can skip to the next step if you like to fly by the seat of your pants.)

3 Tie a knot in one end of the elastic.

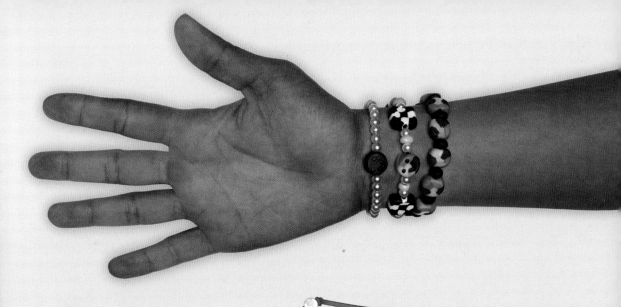

4 Slide on a pearl bead.

5 Add the rest of your beads. At the other end, add a pearl bead and tie another knot in the elastic.

TIP

The pearl beads and the extra knots prevent your beads from scattering if the bracelet comes undone.

6 Cross the elastic strands over and under one way ... then the other way. This creates a double knot.

7 Pull the ends super tight. Trim the long ends, but not too close to the knot. About ½ inch (13 mm) is good.

IF YOUR BEADS GOT SMOOSHED, the hole might not fit onto the elastic cord anymore. If that happens, you can use jewelry-making supplies from home.

Project Ideas

You can make more than bracelets. Here are a few bead-tastic projects you can try with some supplies from home.

PHONE CHARMS
Loop the elastic through your phone case.

KEY CHAIN
Tie your beaded cord to a metal ring.

SHOE CHARMS
Use extra-large safety pins from home.

SUNGLASSES CHAIN
You'll need a *lot* of beads and longer cord.

ZIPPER PULL
Tie a short, beaded loop to the end of your zipper.